IN THE ROOM INSTEAD

Peter Asher

ASHER
SCUNTHORPE   LINCOLNSHIRE

British Library Cataloguing-in-Publication Data.
A catalogue record for this book is available
from the British Library.

By the same author:
Icon
February's Devil
Respect
Gibbering
Eyeless Plaza
The Pointillist Beard
Submarines on Winter Evenings
Poorly Boy Stories
Pig of a Cat and a Kid
Lyrical Mallards

ISBN 978-0-9563282-5-0
Printed in Great Britain by
Arthur H. Stockwell Ltd
Torrs Park   Ilfracombe
Devon EX34 8BA

THIS BOOK IS DEDICATED TO THE DIRECTOR

There's another room, the 'room in the head'.

What keeps mine furnished with tarnished trophies is the chapbook, *The Heights of Wuthering*, published in America by Minotaur Press in 2012. Favourable reviews of collections in small press magazines, and many poems published the world over.

But in that room in the head instead of these, at its centre is the one unblemished trophy – largest by far of the lot, thank God. It's these words of Richard's: "Your poems are fantastic and I love them."

That trophy shines before me in my mind's eye wherever I go, and were it not for it I really do doubt I'd ever go out with confidence and self-assurance at all.

Eight sacred words that justify my being born. Thanks, Richard J. G. Stockwell, master book maker, master archer. Master archer of the syllable to cling to in flight. Straight arrow, with the tell-it-as-it-is true word tip.

PREFACE

How clever the human
spider is.

Eight legs: a left, a right
to scurry away from the light.
Two ears, leg it across unstable
verbal ground to reach dodge
talking morsels of sound
might go both ways but worth a pounce.
Two eyes, to deftly take each step
to find those sights might best
blind it. Two arms to charge
Light Brigade-wise ahead
to grab it all and get shot dead for it.

Spider spiders build webs simply,
to just catch flies.

The human type spin around
big lies, small pleasantries from
deceit-weaving glands in mouths
painstakingly adapted to the opposite task
of catching the spinner out
(as you'll find in these pages somewhere abouts).

How clever is that.

IN THE ROOM INSTEAD

In the room there are
no elephants. Elephants make
their own way to graveyards,
don't need anyone's help
and have no intention of rising again.

In the room instead
there are thick-skinned greyish
contentious questions, dressed as nearly
invisible elephants. Not quite silently
making their way to be born again
in the next ten meetings corollary to this
as the ever thicker growing skin of gnarled
unanswered issues. Looming, like great tree legs
in ominous shadows, shaping across the faces of frowns
by way of tight-lipped grins, the anxious
hand-tugged trunks of chins, eyes unmeeting
and nervous throats cleared fleetingly.

Or better still,
not to die at all,
but wait – vigorously healthy –
outside the walls to throw their token
costumes off, banging knees on rumoured e-mails
and barging one another with bullish
claim and gleeful accusation,
whilst now maintaining complete invisibility.

SEPTEMBER GATES

When my
father died –
it was the
summer holidays.

His old school
playground went
from railings
to infants' wing.

Threw up its
ancient cane and –
in cries of anguish –

Opened its
September gates again.

SEEING THE LIGHT

Those who are
afraid of the dark

Should realise the dark
is also afraid of them.

And if they put the light on
it will see them
and run away.

SECOND CRASS

The wallpaper cried
on the night that he died;
it peeled with the pain of his passing

And the shed stood and bled
with its planks to its head
and its windows it considered slashing.

No more would he claw
with his nails the door
while his brains on its panels be bashing

And the door pined away –
for mahogany, say –
with the new owners' concrete rehashing.

Surprising how soon
a house breaks the spoon
that was wooden and part of the owner

Whose shed's ghost would claim,
whilst the swimming pool sprayed,
such pretensions are incongruous boners.

A SEANCE

Old plumbing
is as good
as a seance.

It's possible
the thumps
are ghosts of
long-ago hand-
washings coming
in from play.

Or the shades
of jugs pouring
tap cold days
out of
hot tin baths.

REDUCTIONS

The sigh that
skips across
many everyday sights,
gaily calling
Mummy and Daddy –

Is the same sigh that
sighs whenever the mirror's
toy-shop window
offers closing-down reductions
on many years' sights ago.

THE SAME LIST

Every generation rises with the forest

    Plays in the meadow
    works in the drainage dyke
    breeds in the sun.

Every generation has every inclination to run

    But stays near the forest
    greying in the meadow
    finishing the drainage dyke
    watching loved ones die in the sun.

Every generation has a single invitation till it's done

    Then rises from the forest
    takes up its belongings
    drags crumpled from its pocket

The same list it'll nail up for the young.

SADLY

Such difference
should be
between children's
wakefulness
and our
awake.

Sadly
they are become
as awake
as we.

THE SCRAPYARD

Evenings
are heaped
the other side
of these hawthorn
branches,

Awaiting the
brown field's mechanism
to press the wrecks
to small convenient
segments of calendar
against night skies.

A FUR OF SHADOW (SORT OF WORD)

There is a word beyond love,
but of love's leading.
A small black creature of a word,
often spied but never heard
scurrying through the reeds of need
on the shores of having been
together for years.

A fur of shadow sort of word,
on the fingers of a couple's first birth,
scrabbling rear of doing without,
hanging about making do for years.
On its back through children going
off to war, or out the door with
family of their own.

Crouching, anxious to the side while
one holds the other tight through smiles
and troubled times. Sniffing their ageing
bones and wondering where it's going.
Small furry creature of a word it is –
knowing both of them have seen it
and let it go for fear it may be just
as much in need of them also
as they of it.

YOU'LL NOT BELIEVE IT

You'll not believe it but
ordinary domestic windows –
not modified unduly – made
the first moon landings
from landings everywhere –
top of the stairs or rough
shed on riverbanks.

Astronauts in pyjamas with their
soft-toy, chocolate-digestive-suited
pilots – or long-ago fisherfolk lifting
off from the smoky hole where
the firelight soared skywards.

Windows; glass-driven or nothing in them,
had boosters for brooders fitted
between their frames –

And the names of those who
undertook the journey are forever
etched on every gravestone
in the world's churchyard halls
of fame; from the Unknown
Soldier to the desert's unmarked
bones – of a nomad –

Though of the craft made of wishes
they travelled in – little may remain
but the dust of the moon to which they came.

THERE'S

Not a point
that can be
made lightly –

That can't become
pointed enough to
do real harm.

THEY DON'T TELL YOU

What the ghosts
never tell you,
as they put on
their robes for haunting –

Is that the one
they hand you – and you refuse –
is bespoke too and surely will fit.

THE HOUSEHOLD CALVARY

Their carpet started fighting
again this morning. Each face
in the plain mat throughout
took sides and piled up and over
the soles of the four feet on it.

A writhing, grumbling, verbal stain
of veiled accumulated grudges,
rumbling, that spread from the initial
subdued skirmish in the lounge,
silently, right up the stairs and into
the south-facing bedroom.

Where the superheroed walls called
to cloths on the floor: "Children;
their needs and routine first!"
When the guard was mounted

(At breakfast, as it always is, every morning,
post the battle) – Dad received (bowed head)
his usual crown of thorn-like design
from the skull-faced stains on the rug
(sympathetic bystanders on the way to the Cross,
veteran members of the household Calvary
in the carpet).

As the children put the scrambled eggs
he'd brought them (bowed head)
down their legs as marks of acceptance
over Dad's respectful surrender –
and he was marched by the youngest,
wanting something – to Mother's reflection,
imprisoned in the blender, where the two of them
serve their life sentence.

THESE TRUTHS

These truths you hold
up to the light
are true.

As long as you don't
hold them up to
the fading light.

Then the light, no longer
in your eyes, no longer
blinds you to the untruth;
truth never hides well enough
for bad light not to shine through.

MUGSHOT

Slamming a snowy fist
down on the county –
the ugly twist that followed this,
given to the throat of an icy road,
was not expected.

Nor the roar of the engine,
floored by a stuck foot,
giving a most unsightly lisp
to the lip of an accelerator's mugshot.

THE HORRORFICE

OK, class, while you're at your best –
get hold that end of the grass and
roll our city back from its roots.
See exposed there; adults not even half
your size in government, justice, work,
play, home and

Horrorfice – the hole there in the middle
where our school is. Note it's left blank
and vacant for a little later when you're
older and the strength to be bold enough
to expose a city to a sun you're young
enough not to wish to own has all
gone and you're

There in the midst of the small, dark
secondary-school part of it. Put it back,
class. I hope you've seen enough already –
not pretty, is it? But do try to remember;
the big problem with the horrorfice is
its unstable ability to blossom forth
from the grass and become your office.

GENIE RUNDOWN

To exorcise broken urban
with rites of refurbishment –
still won't be rid of
          Genie Rundown.

They rub bottles two-thirds full
to fetch him from the space
between the dregs and greasy lip marks
round the rims, enough times
to summon him to render all
amelioration; wined wall piss stunk.

To exorcise well-to-do areas
with windfalls and stock accounts
won't get rid of him either – not
          Genie Rundown.

They rub saucer eyes and glib smiles
with greedy fingers enough times
to fetch him from the vast space
between wanting a pleasure
and getting it in the eyebrow
to hairline wall of wrinkles stacked comb-wards.

Yet Genie Rundown is really
          like Jesus.
He'll forgive – and also, like
the Saviour, his weakness is loving muck
against his better judgement:

As he maintains – you can clean
the surface of walls,
but not even for a moment
the inside of foreheads.

BUZZ IN THE EAR

Words walk horizons further.
Walk the talk and talk the walk –
truly cool they are when going further.

Further than the setting saying
and the going-down of the sundry
superlative's supernova moment.

It's by diffidently asking of itself;
"Is there something further than
the vanishing point at the end
of the tongue's flat earth?"

That some uncertain word
(more overheard than preened
in a certain world)

Takes it on itself to dare to dream
of rising in the morning
as the buzzword with which to be seen

Ties its hitherto ill-fitting syllabic shoes –
straightens its definitions meagre
stood about and yawning queues –
and confidently strides on to take
one's easily impressed by verbal celebrity,
wide-eyed tiny vocabulary, by storm.

HOT AIR

One afternoon, round the hour his wife
used to kiss him home from work –
he overheard thc cokc fire chattering about
their second cat (the tiny triangle
of white on its back to be precise).

His daughter called and agreed
fires shouldn't do that – so with
the old fire gone at last
and new central heating installed –
he said to her how surprised he'd been
when the radiator in the lounge near his chair
rattled on concerning his wife and how
before she died she would wave him goodbye
every morning as he cycled to work.

You can't have a place without warmth
of course – and he resigned himself to
these hot-air ramblings for
a few years more alone – until the night
he gave up on heating when living at
his daughter's; too ill to care for himself –
when the soft-spoken electric fire
of the room to which he kept
bored him to death.

ANYONE WOULD HAVE DONE IT

I reached the market with
the bomb strapped securely in place.
This little boy who didn't
know my face came over
to me, distressed and crying.

I tried to comfort him as best I
could under the circumstances.
He'd lost his mummy and would
I help look for her?

He gripped my fingers as we
searched around, eventually
locating her in a not dissimilar
panic, arms flinging wildly over
by an uncomfortable-seeming policeman.

She hugged her boy. "Praise be
to Allah!" she cried, taking my hand.
I told her it was nothing and
anyone would have done it.

TOUGH CUFFS

Wearing the heart on the sleeve,
it's surprising how tough the cuffs get.

The heart, heavy as it is, the sleeves
won't let it sag further than
to be seen and said of it;
it's an exhibitionist, a diva up its sleeve,
a hysteria of a heart who's craving attention
rules its beating, bleating head.

It's surprising how tough a sleeve can get –
wiping, in a burden-shouldering kind of way,
red watery eyes that seemingly carry
the weight of fifty grieving angels,
sent to sit in sympathy on tiny, cunning
eye-corner biceps – for heavy dramatic effect.

A heart worn on the sleeve believes
in the strength of that sleeve to keep
the heart's chin up, in the end.

PANE IN PAIN

Open a window of opportunity
on hopefully a brighter future,
framed in the aspirational
double glazing of 'at last'
realisation, plus 'can't go wrong'
insulation.

Open a window of folly
it'll shut at speed – guillotine indeed.
So fingers burn between the double
dazing of stupidity seal and crushed
dream seam, as it peels off the idiot
face each sees framed in the shaft
of daft we assumed was light
the other side of the crafty
pane of crass we mistook as glass
in the first place, that the burning
pain is rightly named in honour of.

The corollary maintains; a pain
in the neck sustains, when a weight
of frame remains to bedeck
an unfortunate head and shoulders –
those occasions the window of chance
slams back crash on its arse.

Shatters its glass in troubling
shards of jagged crass problems,
its white-knuckle ride bleeding feet
are barely equipped to kneel upon
to beseech clemency from, let alone
limp across.

TO A TEE

What it is about the mist
is this list of what you'll never be,
that's usually hidden.

That when the mist's done it takes
with it – and you see where the list
has been, a clock with a shock
up its cool digital upturned collar's sleeve.

To the effect saying: "You've got to
get a move on, you're late for work today, mate,
and your fate hangs in the balance of this new
bloke, just started, enthusiastic after your job,
no doubt about it. And you can't blame the delay
for being late on the mist's list any longer,
with its numbering of your misty might-have-beens.

"Now it's gone – taken its fuzzy light
that so brightened items. Till – with far less
perspicacity – you still partly feel the reality only
mist completely revealed, foggy in high definition,
by the dog of a far-off bark in all its shark-stark, sharp clarity.

"And you realise how clearly
the list had you pinned to a tee
by the ogre of a tree. And other
gloomingly enlightening things you'd
never see so uncomfortably, when the sun
is up to no good, because it's not
bright enough for such deeply dark,
blindingly opening-eyed, reflective introspective dejection."

THREE UNIQUE MOMENTS

That voice –
as so often – will
(one quite unique moment)
say the
loved one's name

And stay
open – the voice vulnerable
to the possibility of screaming –
together with its mouth
in order to realise — infinitely
slowly (and another quite unique
moment) –
that the name spoken
will no longer be heard
                    by the loved one –

And for
the first and last time,
that mouth kept open
by the voice which spoke –
                    will swallow –
and bear the beloved name
                    back home.

TO CATCH COLD

Slow may have a
long way to go –
but at least it knows.

Speed is too
slow to catch cold,
maintaining it sees
more of the world.

But seeing
is what happens when

Speed starts sneezing
and sees more from its bed –
at a deeper understood
and faster rate –
than ever it saw speeding.

TOE ROPE

Loose ends again – and in
the blink of the big toe's eye
the toe's snagged – and

His foot's dragged back
to the night of the last snap –
when the rope broke – and

The way to cope is to
walk from her,
step free of entanglement – and

Until then it worked – and
then the jerk again of the
loose end

Tied to the ties;
that end that breaks the tries,
her end that tries them back again – and

Coming from where big toe does,
he can't see a thing,
thinks his big toe's king.

UNBALANCED

How thin-skinned the rain is.
Tough enough to send its manlike
inside into shivers, yet weak at its
drip-droppy knees at sight
of a beautiful girl blue sky
with a lovely sun-sunny smile.

Why – peel the seal on a single
tear of a drop and what the dry find
remains behind is the courage of nothing.
It's all sham and posturing.

And how the rain ever managed to share
the drain of a sea with a land free
of holding itself in on its shores any
more just here, spit its bit for a lake's sake,
or bully a dam into being concrete thug
for a breached bank's flood, is beyond me.

How a soft plop of rain can get
that angry man red it kills with gorgeous
blue crashing waves having a diva day
a hundred thousand, is fantastic to comprehend.

Unless the rain is – unbalanced – essentially
masculine in the pink, but with a sad,
easily moved feminine heart – split in two posturing
(manlike in a very real sense).

Too mercurial to trust – unbalanced – as wet
becomes dust the next moment, one of us in effect.
In that rain's feet is clay soon to pass away
as yesterday's spoilt holiday – just as with us.
Somebody's off-colour wet, wet memories of a dry, dry,
colourless life. Seen through to the end. See through posturing.

WALL WHEEZY

Wall wheezy
bathroom corner,
sick to its tiles' hearts
of seeing life in the raw –

And watching steam dreams
take shape,
go ape,
disappear.

Or worse still – towel down
the hopeless rounds of flesh as found
hardly fit to shadow-box a bit
those troubles hit below the belt
the idle mind that sweats through this.

Only to finish up
back here –

With a wall wheezy
bathroom corner,
sick at heart of steam dreams
manufactured for jeering
needs of cheerily gurgling
plugholes.

WATCHERS

When I'd finished straining;
what I couldn't reach was too
high above the carpet pile for me
to take hold of.

"There's a whole world down here," I cried
thankfully from my chair's stare-watch
deep and safe within the rug as if it were
a nylon thigh my eyes had led me into.

"There's a whole world up here your eyes have
led you into," came the watchful budgie;
parting my patterned-fibre reverie with
a start of honesty from high above me.

"Done hiding?" inquired the light switch. "Turn
him on," demanded the rest of the gloom.
"We will," affirmed the passers-by outside
the room.

"We'll watch when he comes out, see if he
goes in the direction of the school and
our children. So we'll have him pinned
down. Observed for putting away again."

THE WANTED PLANET

Rubbing shelves together;
in the sense of pushing
one fixture up against
another, still allowing sufficient
room for shoppers, but maximising
floor space – is providing more of
a service than ever before to
the environmental cause.

Rubbing shelves together. (To reduce
carbon-inducing friction; this new
quickly disappearing easy-snatch
grip packaging green consumers want –
is quite smashing for
rubbing hands together
in the boardroom.)

We'll disclose why.
Rubbing profits together – wrapped in
a trademark-registered environmental
banner – releases fewer gases from
the masses; who don't exude as much
hot air regarding wasteful corporate
practice any more.

And that's got to be a bonus
for all of us on the face of
the planet: that face displayed
on 'wanted' posters affixed to
asteroids everywhere up there;
with a price on its head
for us to collect.

THE UNREADY

Just deserts –
like something nasty
come out own
mattress.

To dream inside a
pillow forever
would be better, but –

Then – dreaming inside
pillows is only for
the unready;
the unmade
bed of a soul

Whose coverlet's
best left untidy;
orderly rearranging
of, not yet possible.

WHEN

When the cat
puts the door out,
and the dog takes
your bones out for a walk –

They, or what they have
mutated as –
are where your civilisation
                    was
(cat nudges skeletal door
on leaf-frail hinge,
dog walks out with –
          you'd sooner not know) –

Whilst you stare back flat
from off a history scene's
monitor screen
(should they from their
underground disadvantage point
find a way to reconnect a circuit) –

And wonder why
you didn't look after
your little dog and cat better.

WHO GOES THERE?

Two owl pellets lay
in earshot of gunshot,
guarded by silver birch,
as thin as anorexia and
as patchy-skinned.

Skin things preserved in fur
their bones within gullet made
bundles, crop not sea changed
into something worth picking
up and strange.

Enough to take home, open,
see who goes there in
one owl pellet –
the other saved because
it came from where natural
supernatural history makes mystery –
and his Englishness; the teddy-bear-
eyed, magic-necked bird of childhood's
would-be paradise is wrapped within each
adulthood's hazy backwards gaze – opened up
every time it's looked at to reveal
the small tiny bones of picture books.

A SPECIAL MATE OF THEIRS

The central-heating timer
and the bedside wake-call jangle
put on their get-up-and-go sounds
and go fetch the daylight from the local
horizon on the corner of the autumn,
where it joins the main winter.

Once back inside the clearing head
and focusing eyes, both barely adequate
warmth and just enough time,
rub their cold comfort together
in front of the toilet, toothbrush
and breakfast mug (a special mate of theirs).

This typical day of going their own way.
Later they'll set aside a little time
for themselves. Check their relationship's
still right to arm in arm their lights,
click all the bells, for their trip to the corner
autumn in the morning.

WHEN FORGIVEN

Young and old alike –
self-indulgence can become
sole reason for living.

Maybe it's neither body nor soul
that resurrects – but what one
can expect (when forgiven)
is both belly and genitals
to be fitted with angelic wings –

Stomachs and private parts
alike to ply hereafter,
stuffing and rutting
in the bowels of Hell –

Just by confessing
over the plate of chips of our last supper,
a sublimely anorexic Christ –
died for us.

WISE MOUTHS IN A WAX WORLD

To speak
from the profound silence
of listening
is to speak
with the mouth
full of wisdom
and not wax.

To see the ears
in a perplexity of furrowed
wrinkles – such confounded
tangle of brows as to
how to implement wise mouths
in a wax world –

Is to realise
the profound sense
in a sound sense of smell
for detecting
confoundedly bad breath
surrounding resoundingly
impractical words.

THE WIZARD OF LOSS

I don't like speaking my mind
because my mind, like a bed
that's never made up, is even
harder to find free of untidy niceties
when I need it for speaking's
comfortable sleeping.

Speaking aloud; is a sign of being
caught without silence – something
one should never be without, essential
as it is to good conversation.

As for discourse; a horse that'll
run away with your throat to pitch
it and ditch you in the moat
of castle conservatism – sooner than
canter with you on its back, passed
the halls of rant and the barony
of cant – away to the fields of
whatever you say informs barely a day
in the Land of Was where the Wizard
of Loss listens to each breath taken –
where its not expected one repeatedly claims,
"God help me, another breath less to be,
on my way to the end of me . . . that's
why I'm always nervously chattering!"

Somewhere you don't have to say
you want to stay. Somewhere all's
become pure listening.

THE WORK ETHIC

An ethic can adapt,
be modified, construed
and survive for long years
in regular use.

It was always a welcome sight;
the bile in the bath,
things soon to be put to right.

Next step, clear water, not a
trace of currant, chip or liquorice.

Never saw blood, a good job for that,
this shift-rota way of
not getting fat.

To vomit till the teapot beckoned
for me to rest from work a second.

WORLDWIDE WIDE

With the round shoulders,
you get the whole world.

I saw a little man
broader than the universe,
carrying upon his cheap green-
clad shoulders everything life
told us about failure.

Yet that's the trick;
that man's the pick of all
of us – because he knows it –
he's aware an unfair universe
makes a barbell one whole
lifetime thick and no matter
how short it is – man, it's heavy!

Great chunks of reinforced agony either
end, weighted for the brave only
                                    to lift
with a shaft made of solid
dupe that goes right through you.

And it's good some visibly carry it
while the rest see their barbell
laid there and go away
on permanent holiday – working
and enjoying, forever running round
avoiding it lying there, just waiting
for them to trip over it.

Celebrate men and women who are cheap
green-clad and have muscle-less bulging biceps
each side of worldwide wide pigeon-
                                    chested shoulders.

WHY FOR?

A word which the eyes
(shouting, to the mind, as always)
expect to find next in a sentence
they're reading – is missing.

That is silence; to be bamboozled
so the mind caught off balance
by the absence, beseeches the sight
for reassurance – certainty.

It must be just like that –
a silent moment – that moment
the knife is thrust in. Perplexed,
vexed, uncertain; the nearest one ever gets
to silence is the moment after the question is asked.

The mind goes off to look for something
whilst scratching its head. That's the effect
the countryside has on one – something
you never find the why for. That silence –
being left with that 'For why?' you have
to die for in so many left-speechless
                                    ways to answer.

WILD WESTERN

When
too much depends
on things –

Things
depend too much
on too much.

And *Homo sapiens*
are no longer humans,
but *Homo sapiens*.

REALISATION

Some men go out in the morning
and return at night as women.
They haven't undergone sex changes
or been mutated by the latest
scientific advance.

All they've done is realised,
for the first time in their lives,
how unlike their mothers
their fathers really were.

SHOWDOWN

When they grow up
and go from the door –
not living with you any more –
the door goes with them out the door,
closes with them as they close it.
It can be seen following them
down the street, screaming, pleading
for their return home.

You'll see it, can't avoid,
look annoyed – passed all that – seeing as
they've given you a set of these;
the sights attached to a please gun –
a me-please gun – a please-themselves gun, as they did,
as the door always used to please itself,
whether it stayed open or not when they
were at home, swinging with them,
as it did to and fro.

And now they're gone and the trigger is pulled
on the issues they gave you; an exact pear-
handled copy of their selfishly initialled
me-please gun – surely the only thing
they ever gave you of their own.

Go on. Melt it down in the fire of your anguish
and recast it as something different – a please-
you gun to please yourself what you do with it.
Go and have a showdown with the front door,
or saddle up, the two of you, and go out
prairie-ing – anything, even drinking at The
Last Chance surrounded with other doors, is better than
being together alone, sniped at by your own doors.

SOLE EQUAL

At fourteen, I was told
by my teacher that –
I must know it all because I didn't listen.

This echoed my dad,
who often said exactly that
and had since I was ten.

As I grew, my early champions
were proved right, as in every
walk of life I'd run.
I rose to sole equal among mere sequels;
and none stood beside me
on a ladder, or followed, as I
had set unreachable heights for every rung.

Other than – or so I hoped –
for my only son, who at fourteen
showed such intelligence that
he told his teachers he knew it all
and me too. That's when I had to accept the truth,
that he didn't.

SIGNED ORIGINAL

I have a signed original
of tomorrow given me
by today.

It has all the mannerisms
peculiar to the artist –
the characteristic strokes
of the painter's clock
one associates with
my getting up
are depicted in
the depressing colours
of me having breakfast.

And the artist's rendition of
my midday-to-late tea
is a fine facsimile
of what the painter saw
earlier, executed in a
grinding vermilion times before.

While in the corner is my bed
and, upon it, my head in
exactly the same position
the artist caught me for
that signed original
of my birthday card
that's hung beside some more.

SILENT OVATIONS

In the theatre on the corner
the book of the film
was scripted for
childhood acting,
Dad's bit part, and
Mum's starring role.

It's where Dad delivered his
famous Thoughtful Son Speech,
upon my observation I hoped
it stayed fine for the
school trip to Scarborough
when I was too ill to go.

It's where Mum was
tremendous the night Dad
gave her the two black eyes
and where a little earlier
he didn't speak lines
for days on end.

There too I'd lose
my stage nerves,
just outside the theatre
with other child performers.
Offstage like me awhile
from their own silent ovations.

SHUT THE MORNING'S MOUTH

Shut the morning's spoken-for
mouth for it, good and proper –
punched it in the appointment,
with a refusal to keep it.

Did I sulk? Did I not throw
such a 3-p.m. clock arm bending,
as broke the afternoon's resolve
to be any other than
my scowling couch?

Me upon it – a time-ignorant
lout, right up till night approached
to grab my throat with the one
mighty yawn it socked me –
its other dark arm going round
the so slight shoulders
of the fainting light –

To show it
night had had enough
of my posturing.
   Shed no more for
dread of me, those patchy alopecia
traits one associates with balding
day's hair-falling rays,
through thinning trees on edgy,
nervous people fearing evenings such as these.

SELFLESS KNOWLEDGE

You're no longer
as blind as
you'd thought
   they were –
no longer unaware
that they do know
   about you.

Fear strips upbeat –
and you are
   disproportionately
afraid from then onwards,
exactly how much
   they
do know about
   themselves.

THE SECRET

They daren't tell Jesus
        about Christmas,
but speak in whispers
round dark cloud corners
huddled at harp classes.

They don't want Him
        to know their secret,
the truth of it
transpired these Decembers.

Praying with brows knitted,
exchanging anxious glances,
they're hoping that
He doesn't look down.

STREETS CAUGHT IT FIRST

Streets caught it first – picked up
in the crooks of their uneasy curves –
such heavy news as would bend the legs
of a decade, keep its estates at heel,
well behaved with a murder a year
and the added support of its bowed years
beneath a weight of heavy shopping days.

Streets caught kerbs full of unrest – at best,
bodies, at worst terrorist threats. And yet,
still the spring did its thing –
on the ball, dawn chorus and all before
the earliest machete's call.

So no door is blown off its pretty little
unhinged number's head, or is pinged to a
limp-hanging spring handgrip.
For February instead (more regardless than oblivious
to a scaredly staring anxious windowpane,
peering furtive left then right, then above
the imagined frown-browed shelf of the
beyond-the-eye guttering) –

Straps on some buds and leaves, makes it goal
the bull on the target of an early
wild-flower wooded fringe – and springs
a rescue mission. Sunlight to spear
a drive to liberate from fear
the walls in my hall and the despair in here.

SIZE BY SIZE

The first thing the mouse did
when it found me in the trap
was to break off bits of cheese to
feed me; having no idea how long
I'd been caught and anxious, as it seemed
to me, to want to ease my suffering
in any way it could.

When the cat appeared, the mouse put its own
life on the whisker by acting as a
decoy; leading the animal away before
it had chance to see or sense my
plight.

When my wife arrived home, it led her
to the room where it had continued
nursing me, as best it could; the little
thing being unable to spring open the trap
and set me free.

When she saw us size by size,
she promptly fainted
at my small stature beside
that of the mouse.

SOLID FILTH

They pedalled fine ships
to work each day
and home again at evening,
the ships slung
over their shoulders.

Convoys of them; fine
men with the seas
in their bike frames
and generations of
masts and funnels glimpsed
through proudly satisfied eyes
of many a lunch bag's eager aspirant.

Like the miners and steelworkers,
the solid filth of their beauty
was not apparent until
rains washed it silently away
to run in regrets
glimpsed down the faces
of many a shift's windows full
of nervy eye-twitch monitors.

SOMETHING FOR FREE

Of all the places
you could shop that
Saturday afternoon on
Scunthorpe High Street –
the one most
rewarding to visit
was that owned by a
small pied wagtail
pitched about the green
bollards on the
footpath by the pub.

Had you gone inside
you'd have received
a free blessing with
each delight you
took away from
the roofless premises.

You wouldn't make a
better or longer-lasting
purchase that day –
and the price was
so little you
could afford
what you saw.

SOMETHING TO DO

It's something to do,
east to west, easy,
well practised – a job
demanding little by
way of thought or effort.

A rut to a rout;
one sun's foot in front of
another rise to set down
follows Father's footsteps until
something happens to prove
Him right, wrong or fictitious.

It won't be death because
that's simply something to do.

It will be easy and well practised;
a purely routine workout for a
black hole, for instance.

Something to do for a
sky full of lemmings.

SOME OF YORE

Life can't get on with some people.
They're the sort who ask it too many questions
about itself and its motives. They interrogate it;
follow it around with notebooks

Wanting to know why it's
as stupid as it is, has two sexes, but many
others; and why there's rich and poor and they're
both the same in different measures.

When life takes a bath, these people
ask why it's so grubby and stinky and why
it leaves so many stains of one sort
or another.

Luckily for life these people never seem
to get together. They appear to act
independently of one another, though aware
in a vaguish sort of way there's

Others out there like themselves,
not cutting life's corns. (There's plenty here
who'll do the latter; running about after
life, not tracking it down.)

Some people don't work shifts only centuries.
And fortunately for life there's fewer of them
in its hair than of yore. Not ducking,
but hectoring every time: picking up a

Hole in the sky up its filthy war.
A nasty disease on its multinational.
A bad habit from its totally irrational. Or
a platyrrhinian blond(e) its Coptic agnostic multicultural.

SOME MAFIOSO

He'd been a
bad boy all his life,
so before it began
some mafioso got him
first and last by
tying him to a womb.

He stayed tied to it,
but it didn't prevent
him stealing what
education he could.

Some Mafia
threatened him with
a rewarding job
and success.

They gave him a
football team to cheer –
and various women to jeer –
but still he rallied
against and for such
punishments as holidays.

In the end, some mafioso
gave up on him and
with a mind set in
this boot of
cultural concrete
firmly round his neck
and his foot in it
to his eyebrows –
they watched him
satisfyingly drown
in hock above his head
beneath the weight of powder
up his nose.

SOMETHING DIFFERENT

Cogs and wheels,
stanchions –
steeled pieces tempered
with temper's heat
and heart grown colds.

That's old for you –
behind skin's perimeter,
whistles and bangs.

Gangs of cell-tugging
ganglia lug nerve's fibre
to go on producing
or not. Moral fibre
to carry on manufacturing
for the flush and bin.

Or to begin again,
doing something different.

SEEN

Between the garage side and fence
something grows, makes little sense –
unless it's seen as recompense
the narrow gap prides on.

The garage will protect the car,
the fence defends the garden flower –
The long kind space is saving face
For the young tree got it wrong.

STABBING IN PEACE

So peace was declared
and for the first time in years

People could return to stabbing
one another in the back in peace.

STAINS

On the wall of the room
where the suicide bomber was
staining for a while –
were a young couple
and their two children –
a boy's stain and a girl's.

These stains would not have
opportunity to become grown stains –
the stains of man and woman.

This was a pity as these stains are
much easier to wash off than the
stains that corrode a man and
make him an abomination –
a suicide abomination.

Those hideous inhuman stains last centuries
and are always to be seen together
on walls with the stains they deprive
of staining sheets when making babies,
growing old and crying into pillows
the way all human stains
were meant to.

STAR-SPANGLED

The children are Eastern-born
and Western-fed.

They look longingly on
the big red sunset
burgeoning dreams as it sinks
Coke-like in the west.

They want the faded brand names
of their aid hand-me-downs
to be pristine as
those logo colours trademarked
by the late sky.

Already the crescents
are star-spangled
in the children's eyes
long before the mullahs
are blinded by evening prayers.

THE SOUND OF SHADOWS

Shadows of things soon fade,
but not shadows of the sounds
they make – these stay shading,
                perhaps whole lifetimes.

The shadows of the school
are still there every evening
for me to stand in and remember –
but the sounds of that playground
                of fifty years or so ago –
those throw a shadow so long
and all-embracingly never fading.

That Stuart, for one, could sound
out of it in the shade of his voice
                at any moment
from whatever sound he's in the shadow of
                or caught up in now.

And cousin Sandra – she could stop
dangling in the lavatory – the seat
still gently nudging her feet
as she quietly hung there a decade later.
She could erase the shadow of her laughter
as she comes towards me from her classroom –

Simply by stepping out of the shadows in person.

STARTING MY DAY

I always start my day
with a big bowl
of fresh, crackling
demands from others.

Often they're already sweetened
when I get them,
which is supposed to be a favour,
but they always
use too much sugar.

They're on the table,
freshly delivered at the door
most mornings. But I
must admit – though it's
a perverse pleasure – to being
partial to those gushing
regurgitations; warm and

Full of the flavour
of utilitarian purposes
my loved ones
have lined up for me –

When I've fully digested
my bowl of
their start to my day.

STALWART

The blue plastic fragment
probably served in a kitchen
dutifully doing as a piece
of milk jug, fridge component
or chair back.

It's all it knows and can't
give up the way of life
that easy.

The next user probably
knew that instinctively,
took rookish pity with
an eye to utility.

So the blue plastic fragment;
all of a true
old-fashioned English yeomanry-
like four-inch square –
can be seen elevated there
right now.

Part of the purpose-built kitchen
where the young are this moment
tucking into a small furry breakfast,
with a blue plastic main beam
serving stalwart in their nest wall.

(STOP) WAIT

Wait – in its unenlightened
state – waits for itself
to happen.
It doesn't realise
arriving is to begin
to wait again:

As to happen – it only
hastens more fraught
foot-tapping.
But once this is pointed out;
the myth of doing
is exposed as being fallacious
just to bring on more stewing –

Then wait awhile wears a smile,
happily waits in line
without ever asking why
the next "Isn't life great?" is late.

STIFLED

Stifled a yawn
and closed the book;
those last two pages
more boring even
than what came
                    before them.

You could hear
the words writhing
like insects and feel
the vibrations of their
panic as the
covers met and squashed
                    them flat.

I was about halfway
through it.

Next time I opened it,
at those pages in the book
I left off from last time –
the words swarmed, black
and all over my hand
up my arm into my brain.
They seemed determined
to take over the world.

STOOD ON THEIR HEADS

A page of English;
turned upside about
and shaken
to find out
if there's any life
left in it.

And even though
it may be next to death –
at the hands doing the shaking –

If the simple action
of movement up and down
releases one last breath
from lines stood on their heads –
one last meaningful gasp –

Then that's profound
in that
any sound –
no matter how faint,
any language makes –
can turn the whole page around.

STILL WORKING

Love remodels
Death –
in its own image.

It tells Death
to leave those who loved
alone and not
separate them again.

Sunset realigns sunrise
some days after
Death misbehaves –

When one new grave says,
"Good morning" to the yearning that
Love, still working,
has just redefined.

SURVIVAL SUIT

March is
for survivors to
excitedly exclaim,
"Hey, we're still here!"

So you and I,
escapees from the family,
got away
last Thursday afternoon

To join the
hidden others celebrating
sheer stamina
as we drove through

The forest's purple-patched
survival suit, with
the charcoal wear marks
on its many elbows

Aware of
the irony in there,
preparing burrow and branch
for the gene fest to come

Whilst we're unstrung
from its eternal aftermath
a couple of
blessed hours.

THESE SITUATIONS

A blue sky full of secrets
lets an autumn afternoon
in on a few; the biggest of
which – 'Why goodbye to this?' –
is about to be tackled.

For teatime's immediate reaction,
we shall go over to
the clock on the mantle, where
some observations of shadows
will be found pertinent.

Their recent absence
having been missed for
the gravitas such presence
always lends these situations.

ON THE BALL

The quest for eternal youth
means in matters of health,
wealth and happiness –

One must be on the ball constantly.

On the ball,
and yet never be known to dribble.

SUPPOSING

There's a place the world
fixes itself when broken,
as it's been when dinosaurs left it,
giant crustaceans,
great religious leaders.

It's a place where tomorrow
negates responsibility for anything
that went today – looking ahead
at itself from the moment of unborn,
knowing itself will be along soon.

It's the place of strength
to go on and it comes to you
whenever your dinosaur dies in your arms
and you see giant crustaceans
clearing a path, moving sidewards,
as you go forwards, supposing you know
what they're doing,
as great religious leaders are parting
like seas to get out your way.

SUNDAY SCHOOL

The river puts its hand in his and
he puts his trust in us,
strangers to the room.

He doesn't work so the river
asked him to take care of it.
There's badgers come by night and
kestrel chicks on shelves in boxes.
Protected breeding couples walk here
and live there.

Jason smiles lopsided, like
a landslip on a sunny day.
A knowledgeable child of
about twenty-three who'll never be
a protected breeding couple.

After half an hour he leads the river
to the door for home time
and, with his gentle landslip smile,
he instructs us to drive back safely.

I feel as if I'm walking out
the school gate at fifteen for the last time.

SURE-FOOTED

When going means leaving
and not leaving to go
just down the road –

A certain sure-footedness
walks all over uncertainties –
an old curtain becomes
a definite turning taken
for the best.

It's with age that,
looking back, one sees
how sure-footed
that first going was.

But not so
those new curtains
and disasters they so often
foretold.

SWALLOWING

There's a lump in
the throat of time
at times when it swallows.

Accounting for its passing
as quickly it does;
out and away from places it

Caught up with you in. Till
all you have is
the memory of it, so moved.

Which is quite moving as it
causes you to swallow hard,
recalling your moment together.

SUBSIDENCE

When a house subsides,
it doesn't collapse in the centre
so the roof falls.

The walls don't come down.

A tiny crack in someone's dreams –
that might have gone unnoticed for years,
apart from the odd passing shrug –

Eventually becomes a great fissure.

And the ground beneath
any number of feet –
caves in.

STUCK TOGETHER

It seemed a
long way to write,
words being perishable
in the warmth
of an addressed envelope.

I sent them first class.
They weren't important,
knowing that
when they were undone
at the other end
they'd be stuck together
in an unpalatable mess.

But it seems she tried them,
having more stomach
for such things than most.

When she phoned,
my ears stuck together
and neither floss nor favour
from her as regards freeing them
came between us.

SYMPHONY OF SEAS

On the brass
of leaves –
the wind's
lips play;

Autumn's piece:
'Symphony of Seas'.

Strange title this one,
for one seemingly
so earthbound –

But to the waves,
in strains of trees conducting –
dewy-eyed and misty-mooded –

The land recalls
days
when it was a seafarer –
long ago –

And all its creatures
swimmers,
and all its rivers
in its belly
waiting to be born.

OLD NICK

Though Nick's brought
the walls down easily already –
he hurls himself
at the wallpaper,
trying to rip it
off its whirls and squiggles
(a pattern's saved me so often
from a fate worse than
broken concentration,
i.e. bad writing).

Neither is Nick strong enough
to move the picture, framed
for blameless huntsmen to go a-
hunting soothing fox-free country –
nor the glaze eye plaque's lines
to any old mother (but still
a comforter to any old son
or brother under siege conditions).

Such that when Nick puts his
Kalashnikov-strength music
campus killing full on – no doubt
with the same intent to cripple
reason – it can only
hurt the poem if the poem
turns its back full on
and runs away from
this cacophonic of a noisy neighbour.

OLD FRIEND

The light goes on:
old friend, there
to help change
the baby.

Little does she know
what the light's up to –
given half-life chance:

Conspiring the murder
of her son (soon as
opportunity comes along) –

Together with the plutonium
it got the idea from.

OBSERVANCE

God gave
the silence of the socket;
the hand descending
with the plug's blessing.

Sacrilegious
not to observe nightly;
this touching of
the floor's forelock
to appease Electricity,

No matter how arthritic-y
the observance gets.

OK

The man with a lisp
showed his identification
upon asking.
      It was obvious
he wasn't the gasman
or anyone demanding money.

We showed him in and
while we prepared the coffee and
biscuits, he rolled up the
carpets and cleared off with
a van-ful of our home.

He took no money and in
many ways this seems a
fairer more equitable way
of paying bills than an
expectation of cash.

I only wish I'd noticed
who he was from.
In due course no doubt we'll be invoiced.
As I say, it wasn't the
gasman. He did have the
lisp, however, so if he comes
to you, remember he's OK.

OCCUPYING
(THE BEST POSSIBLE EMPTY SPACE)

Once – I deliberately
thrust a hand inside
the empty space
surrounding the man –

And immediately felt embarrassed
that others were watching
the hand take the hand
of a slow-moving,
slow-thinking outcast.

Only took it the once, however –
as he never stopped talking,
holding on, gratefully acknowledging.

And I realised how
the outsider with so much inside
occupied the best possible
empty space outside –

So we wouldn't have to be
embarrassed by the emptiness
inside of us
and the embarrassment outside.

OH NO – JUST

A covenant of
old terraced houses
prowl their street
by evening light –

Roof gutters – slightly
drawn down – frown
shadows the facades
inhabit – cloak-like

Or monk-like,
more like –

In the dark habits
of the dark fraternity
of the curtained-eyed.

Though not unpleasantly
oh no –
just bent on taking

The nightly rolls
of their human victualled souls'
room-interior rituals
(as ancient shared histories
between venerable terraces),
across the street

Rolled beneath the arms of black-clad eaves
one robed monk to the other.

ONCE FABRICATED

Once these terraced houses
cycled to labs each morning,
their doors calling to one
another – when 'brother'
meant more than the kid
you were jealous of for
your mother's affection.

From simple ingredients; like
regular bedrooms and shift-
precise bedtimes, these houses
synthesised birth cries
to build whole families.

Under no-nonsense conditions,
properly prepared autumns and
winters made tin-bath-cold
firesides and doorsteps for red-
lead front step and sturdy
sandwiches alike.

The conditions may have been
clinical – but it's surprising;
once these houses took off
their lab coats –
just how lovingly fabricated
were the bedtimes, bedrooms,
tin baths, families and firesides.

ON THE FACE OF IT

The hands on the face of
Grandfather's house
are slowly ticking round.

On the face of it, the dial's
doors and windows are timeless;
the brickwork wound by
decades of Grandmother winding
up Grandfather,
so's the numerals got repainted
regularly enough on the face of it.

But the inner workings are
defective and have been since the
day Grandfather's
time was no longer his own;
so that those young hands moving
seconds on the face of it are
become gnarled and tarnished with
wearing too many faces out,
for the children of their mother
to tell the time by.

None of us really deserve a
good time
piece and all of us put the
hours on and take them off
to someone else's random seasons.
That is why the hands at the
face of my house are
wound only by myself; my
wife and children's inner windows
being of little concern
on the face of it.

ONE OF THOSE

At kick-off
I'd no idea who
pumped the day up,
or who paid for
Yesterday to occupy
the stand behind
the away goal –
while Today had
the home.

At half-time, I'd
seen enough to know
who was going to win –
and by change of ends
I resented greatly being
one of those who
had to subsidise
their ticket.

As they were
walking off at
full-time I'd
still no idea
who pumped it up.

ON OCCASION

Nothing fades like
a fake. Care
must be taken
when removing
a person's shadow,
that the person
remains intact
on the wall.

So's the
mind can shorten
them to nothing
at all.

With the shadow,
folded and put
away to lengthen
over time,
the real is preserved
and fake destroyed –
though it has
been known
to work the other
way round on
occasion.

ON BOARD

Today pays
yesterday to get on board
for some of those sailing in chairs,
paddling tea with spoon oars.

It does it morning, just as
yawning sets sheets to masts
about to dress in the unfashionable
pullovers of old age's flags.

Yesterday has ports of call
for all stained-carpet floor sailors
in such places.
Places where today pays yesterday
to get on board.

ON THE BALL

Those who would live forever
must be on the ball constantly.
Every flu jab is to be laid
claim to, every epidemic
clambered over to the nearest
course of antibiotic.

Each book of fat cutting is
for digesting to the bone,
all accidents shunned, all
crowded places circumvented,
all risks circumcised. All
invitations scrupulously sieved
for the safest.

Those who would live forever
must die forever. Consigned to
and assiduously timed by the doctor's
pressing appointments schedule –
they must nevertheless be moved –

If not by beauty, then to the
sewerage works of their preoccupied
personal infinity of useful product;
for the good of all and the land
they so wish never to leave behind
to muddle along on its
own without them.

OTHER SIDE OF A MAINSTREAM

Equipped only with a licence
the boyish purposefulness of
exuberance sanctioned,
at my lad's pleading,
at the court of
daft-hearted dads –

Sighting the law of averages
on not getting nicked for
being without a provisional –

Choosing to live
the other side of that
mainstream
whose fear skulks in rear-
mirror imaginings,
turning white vehicles
into police cars –

We took that risk . . .
and ran wild and erratic,
welcomed into
Sunday's outcast band
of brooding central car parks,
empty of responsibility
to anyone . . .

For his very first driving lesson.

OPENINGS

The bells will not ring
through streets crying,
"Coronation! Coronation!"
Flogging banners,
pushing flags of 'One Nation' –
ropes pulled down joyous
like the chains of old-
fashioned toilets celebrating
good openings.

The bells have lost
the thrill of mornings,
of togetherness within God's
mighty Norman spires.
And though they'll still
go on forgiving the godless dying,
the loveless their septic weddings –

Its solicitors' bells keep ringing
upon VE day's coming
so very often nowadays,
celebrating fiscal openings
within perfect closures to
string-pulling on behalf of
mourners the world over.

The rest is largely silence
from bells grown fat and pompous,
inclined to liking the indolence
of museums in America, which all
bells aspire to – the easy life
with a plague and the patent
crack up the middle. What a liberty,
what a ding-dong proof parody
of glorious past openings!

ON THEIR BEHALF
(THERE'S A CONTRACT OUT)

Unease: to learn nothing
but unease would be
easier by far than
to have to feel its fingers
wrench your ears open,
once you're aware they're
insinusnaking towards you
through the carpet
when you sit down – if you're
lucky – having come through
home's door.

If you're lucky – ah! double-
edged sword. For – unease
will slam the door
behind you; great brawny
portentpaws slugging you
up against the wall –
interrogating heart valves
it pins there by heart's corners,
in a corner – to make it bleat beat
faster what it wants you –
screwing its face into yours.

Unease: snarling how
you shouldn't have
come home without the dawning
fearful notion issued –
and on their behalf –
it's not going to let it happen.

OUR BROTHER

I went to the gutter and found that some other
had picked up our brother and claimed
Samaritan's honours – while I had to borrow
a chair for our brother to faint.

Samaritan's glamour brought people to clamour
for more from this star of the street,
so I was directed and soon had collected
some cash so our brother could eat.

The girls kissed Messiah, who spoke of desire
to the audience wrapped where they stood.
Samaritan preached as if born to teach,
as if born to make Hollywood.

And I was disgusted and my glasses got busted
by the crowd who gathered to hear,
and I fell to the ground and Samaritan found
another excuse for the cheers.

ORNAMENTAL PEBBLES

Some of the ornamental pebbles
reminded the little man –
with the wild beard that's
forgotten him – of dog biscuits.

The beard is largely in charge
and makes him get down on
all fours, with the clothes tired
of being ownerless and caring
for themselves.

The clothes are hungry and start
to nudge the pebbles
as if trying to find the most nourishing
morsel of them.

People pat the little man's head
and feed him pennies for the cheapest
dog meat he can find.

It is a good thing there are the people
as shiny-polished as ornamental high-street pebbles,
for those who know better than us
do not like the lazy beards
of wild-running dogs not fit for kennels.

OR CAN DO

Premature youth –
afflicts old folk
of eighteen.

It's so unlike premature
ageing's youthful exuberance,
overdoing the past
with the sheer force
and energy
of the welcome given it
(over-fixing the spot
on the carpet for hours
at a time, so taxing
to those who can't keep
    up with it).

But premature youth turns
souls to stone (or can do).
Shuffling a self-interest, the virus
wizened to a standstill of enjoyment,
good prospects, or even less mobile
      static
       indulgence.

Thus the premature-aged,
knowing how to be young,
thankfully keep us on our toes.

OPEN WINDOW

The provincial
(would-be)
poetry outlet,
Open
Window,
rejected the
sparrow's submission
received this morning.

The editor
(at the kitchen sink
of literal and metaphor,
washing his hands of
it already)

Dismissed
the bird's offering
for a piece
of noisy modernist
rubbish,
submitted by the
tube to work.

PENCHANT FOR FRIENDSHIP

Bronchitis was good at friendship –
the old steel-town cough had a real
penchant for it.

Bronchitis brought people together
under the umbrella of the shift
bike ride – and brought nights around
to a new-found sense of personal worth
and confidence; seeing street light weren't
leaving by daylight; the smogs holding
hands with the dark.

Only as antibiotics showed a real hatred
for pockets of phlegm did bronchitis's
altruistic spirit desert – reluctantly withdrawing
the embrace of its spit from the pavement –

So that later, when soot from smoke's lungs
had been coughed up – technology slapping its
back to loosen it – steel making became
as mucus-free as one of those rubber chests
used for teaching purposes.

By then, bronchitis was more than ready
to pack its diseased air sacs for the centres
of hard-drug consumption – where it wasn't
so much friendship that motivated it – as genuine
pity that the new ways had introduced such shit.

THE GOOD

Given that reasons are to be seen
on every tree – the eye is defied by mere lifting
of a leaf to peer beneath in sceptical
disbelief at what the third eye (half asleep)
tells it just might turn out to be,

God, in effect – in the bud, chewing his cud –
waiting for us to piss off and look.
Seize the opportunity to see how the cow
in the field next to this, the wood
that seals years up in rings –

Are the very cud and muck of all the good,
coiled to spring the next spring into summer.

MEANING?

The word 'faith'
is chasing its meaning.

Its meaning is such
a naughty child that
the well-disciplined
kid of the word 'chastise'
(a prefect meaning if ever
there was one)
ought to have a severe go at
such a naughty offspring.

Now. The next meaning is
neglected. Its word doesn't love it,
won't recognise it as its kid
any longer and would rather
go to a gay march any day than
take responsibility for its poor,
ragged firstborn.

OATES

From how many homes go forth
those intent on dying
daily – as in legend?

They will save the home
by going forth; save by dying
in the birdsong, losing their way
in the goings-on of sparrows –
and so-doing, coming-home spirits

Refreshed to face it all again:
the intense cold (to give of themselves
by giving up to others) – the emotional
starvation, the mere subsistence on the daily
round's meagre rations (to give of themselves
by giving in to others).

May their legend also go on forever.
For it is they – though absent in their sacrifice –
and almost in their presence – they
who hold the tent together.

PAYING

I have never forgiven
the rain – nor the children
in its pay.

That day I was going home from hospital
when the rain put on
such display of hatred against me.

I was well and going home and it
wanted me dead upon the table
and had been thwarted by the surgeon.

And as for those two children
(paid in rainy ways, I dare say,
for wanting to keep me there) –

With taunts of "Ally, Ally, Astor"
so Mum and Dad wouldn't be able
to drive faster than the rain allowed.

I've often wondered if they're proud
of the memory. And what the rain's
way of paying could possibly be.

THE PHANTOM PILGE

On the line that leads from Ferret's Leg
to Ostrich-upon-Pud
the ghost of Wilhelm Sootshoot Pilge
does roasted owl with spuds.

The phantom poacher of Snot's End
as local legend bends
will choose the barn as just his cairn
and stoke it cigarettes

To choke a filthy feather on
until its boggles belch
and when each dead is round his head
he'll boil them all in squelch.

So be a blighted person well
and keep your gizzle home
and do not venture after dark
near Pretzil-in-the-Loam.

For should you cross the phantom Pilge
beware, behest, bequeath –
he'll leaven you in stock of fowl
and serve you up as beef.

PERFECT HAVE-NOTS (DONE TO A TURN)

A spite wing violation government
(a volition of like-minded hearties)
secures its terrace ticket winded economy
by cutting its debt to the poor
to a minimum.

This it achieves by mischief handkerchief
to the TV screen's grief it causes
opposition left cling parties.

And by cooking books so have-nots
are done in a slow oven (coalition gas
mark; isn't it fun being the ones
to do away with welfare states).

Until browned off enough to not care
any further how many shares they're
cut into by a celebrity-driven cool
country, bites them in two with every
greedy Olympics' wet dream.

PICK

Pick . . . Austin, Singer,
    Fiat and Ford
In jars in a showroom with no one on board
but dust in a summer sun, steering through panes
and dusk in a winter that drives down the lanes.

Brassed and they're banded like fine instruments,
which now play the jam jars the vintage are sent
not down those lanes where old summers would ride,
but where lights in a showroom take dust for night drives.

PICTURES OF SORT

Pictures of sort
cleverly drawn
by curtains whose cords
trace speculative thought
on insides
of evening.

THE PHOTOCOPY

The new gives the old year
an album of scraps
that it can look back on
for a few days, perhaps
bound nicely with twelve months
neatly paragraphed
and an index of names and events.

The old year with tears
down each of its days
will accept the gift
with a bow and a wave,
for photocopying,
then bend to its grave
but it makes sure the copy gets sent

With pencilled injunctions
written so there
can be no more mistakes made
by subsequent years –
to the new year, who's careless
being so young, I fear,
and it loses the copy it's lent.

THE PILE OCEAN

As the pile ocean gets wider
it gets thinner – the pitfall
passage more apparent.
The light is also more watery.

There are perhaps two cave-like doors,
yellow rising shores (sometimes blue-
emulsioned, sometimes papered flowery).
Fewer voyages are undertaken –

The frail-framed craft
taking all the blame
for rugs having got too much
to navigate.

POCKET WISE

There's no pocket
like an old pocket.
It's seen good times,
bad times
and you can't turn it
inside out any longer
with those
little indiscretions still
trying to be younger
or better than you
really are.

CHOP CHOP

In a world of virtual
boys and girls –
virtual games with all too
real names can be indulged in.

Living sniffing another's trivia
is a means of sticking
a keyboard finger up
a bantering screen's inferior
and licking it.

It's a taste one recognises
as virtually one's own
and so it's a short text hop
from the smartphone-shaped
execution block to losing real heads.

RENDERED

The crest
    of a day
crashes down
    on the hours;
rendered flat
    for a moment,
then another
    dawn's seconds
tower upwards
    into minutes;
surfing towards
    sunset
and a shore
    pebbled with seasons.

PLC

The Spitfires he flew were dispensable to the defence of this nation.
The NHS that grew out of it is dispensable to this nation's health.
Businessmen and shareholders are indispensable to the wealth
of machinations that run the nation's stealth.

Having just got past the celebrations for a new thousand years of
unmitigated spend, Lease-Lend and magisterial despair,
he died of flu-related syndromes on the floor there, outside
the ward where an indispensable bed couldn't be found;
an expendable death gone to expensive ground.

Sometime before and after, a fly-past of indispensable
preserved Spitfires had flown their expensive, irreplaceable
tribute, over a grateful stock exchange in commemoration of
fifty expansive years post The Battle of Great Britain PLC.

He will be buried with full honours by his wife's
younger sister, some Tuesday afternoon beneath
a nation's heedless mud.

POINTED

By stretching a point –
the hopeless listener's breaking
point
and stretched point's harping-
on point –

Converge in a mutual
stretching of nerves,
beyond breaking point.

Once reached, the two have achieved
a breach in words – a stasis;
where silence, if not solid golden,
is as tense as tensile metal –
as cold and as stretchable –
filling the void like an expand-
ing universe.

Until a point is reached
(dilating stasis having conflated
two spreading sulks till one
brood touches a nerve and breaks
it into words) when it's time
to stretch a point again and break
more jagged nerve.

SPOILING THE ROCKERY

Our garden has more owners
than flowers. It seems to belong
to the world. One supreme creature
from each territorial species lays claim to it –
including a human – yet not one is aware
the others share that ownership with them.

Too many cooks spoil the rockery's broth –
maybe. Or could it be they make it into
something tasting of victory? But how pyrrhic
can you get when the cat is defeated
by the latest young pretender?
Same with the old blackbird done down by a brutal
yellow-billed usurper. And the neighbour moved in next
door, whose hi-fi roars not only king of his back-
yard, but my jungle too.

Whether to cheep, speak, click or squeak –
we come into being with nothing
and go out of it with less – even the innate
anticipation of a full life ahead having gone.
And as for the time between – nothing
but a series of shared lawns – and an illusory
fight to make all of them one's own.

RE-COLLECTS

Blue tit caught in a crosswind;
halted on path, falters a few seconds.
Re-collects: looks on on fence.

Small boy caught in a crosswind;
halted on path, falters a few seconds.
Re-collects: looks on on mother's hand

At blue tit looking back
at boy looking back.

The bird re-collects – it's not the bird's
purpose to recollect, ever. It is over;
the moment is over before it began.
Nothing came of it that the blue tit
remembers and what it did with it
was simply to move on alone.

But the small boy will – hopefully –
much, much later re-collect to recall
the crosswind that caused paths to cross:
what became of it; what he did with it
and where the bird and him went with it.

PRACTICALLY DEAF

Words must be
good with their hands
(lips, just handy) –

That's the purpose
of sign language.

Ears lost hope?
The hand drill's
air-bit, you'll see, will
cope:

Making holes,
meaning screws into
and out of.

THE PUSHER OF THE DOOR

Having pushed the creaking air open
enough to slide between trees and houses –
whilst tainting the grass with dog dirt –

Unseen, clearly seen by all that is hidden,
makes its way unbidden through lives
it'll encounter any given day.

On its way towards the darkening space
between houses and trees, pulling
the creaking air closed behind it as it goes.

PLUS AND MINUS

March and the earth of the field
has ticks upon it because
it's a good field.

Ticks, under the auspices
of pigeons from the wood,
come to mark it
grey of official feather.

Each bird is a tick from
a car window. The next Land Rover along
will mark the field a minus:

A good field but in need
of a break next year.

ALBATROSS

Picks up by
seat of pants –
then surrounds
neck.

Great metal albatross
(commonly called 'the car')
around prey's shoulders.

THE WINDOWPANE PAIN CRAFT

Strapped into a chair by misery belts
on buckled-down cares –
in front of a window – to hopelessly go
where no given-ins have dragged
themselves before.

My windowpane craft and I,
slimmer's Coke powered by streets, houses,
distance and sky –

Gather speed towards inner cries for help
(or other such spaced-out clichés)
to ply despairing dreams of ever writing
a half-decent line. Searching for it.

I know where we haven't yet tried;
the small white yappy dog over the road,
that yelps at passers-by and is always being
told off by its owner (but never dries up
regardless).

Could be there's a verse there that's
never been gone before if I grind
my sad windowpane pain craft,
through this long clock, clock long,
long, long clock, everything is ultimately
pointless, barking-mad universe,
black hole for clichés warp-speed bold
                              driven afternoon.

Where a noisy Scottie* makes the only
sense at all – if only it discovers
the lost planet of the possible poem.

* our Scottie; of Scottie dog, but also wordplay on the character, Scottie
out of TV's Star Trek. First series.

THE PLAN

From the mind of woman
to the mouth of man
they take their
                instructions
and do what they can.

Then woman thinks again
and alters her plans
and the mouth of man
                goes, "Yes, love."

THE PIRATE

In the land
of the timed –

The one-eyed clock
is king.

And as I
was always looking at it
with one eye –

It became such a
pirate over me that,
when it came to collect –

It was its
Jolly Roger they
wrapped me in.

THE REMAKE

Opens with a priest,
much respected. Blocks of
Berlin Wall are being crated
by freedom's architects
to sell off as past civilisations.

The old priests called over
to one brick in particular,
with crude carvings of figures
he, squintingly slow, understands
as exhibiting the heavenly gesture
of shaking hands.

The wall is quickly disappearing
as the priest looks up from
the find to find
hordes of figures coming towards him
from the other side, arms extended
in gestures of friendship,
brickwork no longer intervening.

It closes with the priest, demoniacally
quick, understanding the figures
in the carving are grabbing him
by the throat, to upend and shake him
in order to exorcise his pockets.

THE RIGHT THING

Setting off for the North Noise,
we expected to find the Wall
of Silence, about where the Small
Talk ended, and taking the Sides
of Dislike, surrounded us.

One brave din, disillusioned with
all of us going up Sulking,
took it upon himself to do
the Right Thing alone.

The Right Thing, looming before him,
he said,
        "I am going out awhile –
then there'll be more quite to go
around for a bit."

We never heard from him again,
but a note was found, together
with his denture fixative,
where he'd tossed his teeth
over the edge of the Sick

Of Words Echo Chasm. There was nothing
written on it, so, as you'd suppose,
Our Tears flowed and we wailed
and rent our vowels
at the way such a large piece
of paper had to die a virgin.

PREVENTABLE DEATH

The little
things;
so small
your life
   swallows
   them –

Can lodge
   in
   some
essential
organs.

You
can die
from them.

PROPERLY ADDRESSED

Look to see.
Doesn't matter how
you look to look;
what look is 'in'
(how you look to appear
        when looking) –
appearances are not seeing . . .

But look.
Look to see . . .

For that is dressing
all addressing properly.

PROFESSIONAL SORE SPOT

Your sense of superiority
and discontent
wearing the glove-like habit
is being picked at
and unwound
by your sense of
irritation and contempt for others.

When the natural
and unsoiled humility underneath
is finally exposed,
a sore spot, like
those you caused
whilst patronising the inflamed areas
of others, will open up
on your vulnerability too.

PULLING . . .

Does adversity bring together
two people whose relationship
severed?
I would say it depends on whether
adversity
severed their lives.

THE READ AND THE FLEE

The hidden agenda's hidden veranda
sicks out like a ram
for those who can see,
and those who have built it
know just how to tilt it,
with its harassing cargo
laid on you and me.

For the hidden agendas
are made by their vendors
to be the lenders of cargo,
justly – quite unintelligible
(as small print is eligible
only for those who
don't read but agree).

And the hidden agenda's hidden veranda
sticks out like a bastion
of fidelity, and those who
have built it know
just how to silt it,
so the shingle when tilted
drowns all in its sea,

Of harassing cargo; shall-nots and embargoes
unless you've forage, whose status is key,
to an open veranda
where tilters don't pander
(for there's no
small print heaped
on the read and the flee).

HIS KIND OF ALCHEMIST

As a life the colour of blood-spattered earth
put through a blast furnace where he served it
after bringing it home from the trenches . . . well,

As a life – when it ended the last thing they
expected to find amongst his personal papers (cuttings
of local team supremacy, Maureen's wedding, odds
and sods on the neighbourhood) was a notebook –
quite a joke book really as they'd never imagined
him a bloke of literary pretensions.

But surprisingly erudite, his spidery lines defined a kind
of 'in spite of book'; concerning his thoughts on the art
of turning limbs in mud into golden life – without
adding watery whys and acid enquiries from
irate parents about their blemishless offspring fighting
in the wrong sort of nasty mountains where even poorly
equipped guns would need counselling afterwards because of
the naughty government.

Notes about an alchemy of doing it because his kind of alchemist
always have – using dirty jokes, well-observed minutes' silences,
national-service kisses on Cold War platforms,
marriage, cycling to work on shift after shift, having kids,
paying ticket fines –

Pushing on with cauldrons full of daily horrors like those
base elements tedium and boredom as a way of transmuting
lost-in-combat or crippled comrades into bog-standard gold
ordinary working-class hard-as-ingot upright-stacked
exemplary lives – in memory of the fallen and those who go on:
because going on is so important, transmuting falling into priceless.

IN THE DARK

Your cows are burnt
and are a breed of phoenix.

Each day carries on on the grind
of cog and oily rag of information
technology at its innovative, Jobs
intuitive finest.

The sun, run off its feet by ten,
is on red.

You don't get much warning,
at work most days warming.
You are both going down.

Run the lights, no one's about.
Someone shouts that you could even police
your own cows if you so wanted.

Through the window the horizon
is angry at a sky that grasps it
by the neck and wrestles it, much effort,
out of the ring both of them.

A few gods step uncertainly,
furtively look at one another
and depart with large trees
up their sleeves only you can Braille-
read in the dark.

PEARLS FOR EYEZING

Being rather old-fashioned, fir trees still
make slides of scattered ashes, in a fathomed
five reminiscent, conic act of kindness.

Employing a technique of dragonflies – those
whys and wherefores misleading sight into
believing they somehow modify light.

For remembrance purposes – pearls for eyezing,
as it were, over spots urns turned up
upturned in. Just a little dash and dapple added.

And there one has it; played upon the mind by
shadows spines projecting memories on pines – one trunk
passing images to another in a veiny bark, full sepia colour.

I was watching slides of Uncle Albert lurch from fir
to fir today. Nice to know he can be his shadow
as lasting as that now though.

Since Auntie Iris's beckoning
on the parson to chuck his dust
on the scullery floor of the wood –

Carve a cross in him and leave him,
his every own cremated Freemason
become vampire – harker of the dark

Dusty arms surround fir cone,
biting wind and all.

PUNC

If I stay on the
inside long enough,
words will become
my jailer.

They'll patrol, punctuate;
interrupting my sentence
for any possible breakout
of meaning doing time.

If so – when you visit,
smuggle inside something
I can chew over and
spit out.

Something with real
stops and pauses
punctuating like bolts
the thin icing disguised
as verbal spanners for
tightening common platitudes.

With that I could
free my syntax forever.

HAY HAND

A field caught
hold a kid's
imagination –
and dragged him,
kicking and gleaming,
hand in hay hand,
through the hard
and barren parts
of childhood.

The kid grew up,
slowed down and hardened off
and let go the hay hand,
which raced ahead
outside of his head without him.

They met again –
as prearranged –
on a long ramble of a day
in old age;
and kicking and gleaming,
hand in hay hand –
they ran through his childhood.

HAVING NONE OF IT

The crying hand
rubbed an eye –
the eye drew back,
wagged a lashed lid's
scolding fingers.

The hand blinked –
opening wide its palm
                gazed,
                   then knuckled
                a frown
as to why the eye
refused to close its eyes
or sympathise.

HOLDING BACK

We were always
held back by you;

At the seaside
sat in the car,

On the pier we never
got to walk along,

The shops we
only just reached.

The countryside felt our eyes
but not our feet,

Now you're in front of us
everywhere we go.

HAMLET'S REVENGE
(AGAIN AND AGAIN)

And who shall
avenge for me
across the grave?

Surely – not you,
Father, though experienced
in losing me my battles
when you couldn't win your own.

It's all, I deduce,
a matter of trust and no
ghost is reliable enough –
so don't trust me, my
son – but lead your memory

Away from me to some sympathetic,
mortgage-paid battlement,
to warm toast soldiers
and gullible kin.

For a seance
on the carpet,
with your
grandchildren's teddies
and my photo,
tapping messages.

HALF VAMPIRE

They put the light on outside so the door
casts no shadow when opened
(half a vampire to whatever teeth
await within at half past three
in the morning).

They don't see its brief, equivocal
cloaking shape, as if undecided
whether to elicit street lighting's
absolution for its kind, protectively
dropped, tentative about their backs
as they close the door behind them.

Half vanquisher, it rushes after,
attempting to tell them, firm lock
and unlikely to be ignored alarm clock –
beware the fangs of dawn – this moment
bravely hid and secured from the day door's
coffin lid they'll be all too eager
to be bitten by and hasten inside
as usual to die.

PUPPED

Mr President is in trouble tonight –
Jack should have phoned but didn't and she
feels it's him to blame going back to that summer recess.

Mr President is preoccupied tonight and
far too busy to feel resentful, blamed unjustly
just like when Alice got crazy over the dog
as if it was his fault it pupped early whilst she was away on business.

In tents under stars, in holes and dugouts
with even worse woman, Jack will be smug tonight
camping with his cronies
putting one over again.

In tents under stars the other side of the world
tonight, people like Jack will not know about
canine impetuosity and
Mr President being father to the nation in times of crisis.

IN THE LONG SUN

A field:
steeled to yield
in its own good time
and an entity fake day makers
oughtn't to tamper with.

So they did:
naturally unnaturally, stretcheth seed
and pulleth weed and feedeth anew
to such extent the sonic seed speed
of field was greatly exaggerated,
accelerated beyond the sound barrier
of meadow pipit and happy cricket.

Speeding careering, driving seeds
beyond the weed of sound –
breaking the per-pound barrier
with sonic boons beyond the range
of human shelf life.

In a long sun-short box-office run
to the fossilised dung of shoppers.

IT'S A PITY

It's a pity the country
should he caught up in this –
towns sobbing, tears rolling down
windows. Gone on ever since
the first rough hut felt gutted
enough to sob its fires out
from the hole in its roof.

It's a pity this sobbing must
soak the robin and the deer
in the wood – though as compensation,
when the room in the house smiles,
there's a warm glow where the deer stood.

It's a pity the country
should be subject to
such fluctuation – does it no good;
just brings the blue and pink of curtains
to cheer the rainfall up.

IT'S OK TO HOLD

Global warming goes
to the fridge in the sun
for an ice age to cool itself.

And that's what
colder winters are about.

Doesn't deny the 'fact';
'Earth is warming at
an alarming rate.'

And that it's OK
to pretend the frozen river
is just the tip of
a subcutaneous thawing
iceberger.

INCIDENT

I have contacted the police
who thanked me for
my concern and solicitude,
together with the get-well
card.

HEART OF STEEL

Between two rivers, roughly,
and two hills forming a plateau,
sort of, where one stops for breath
before becoming the other –

In that breathing space,
pausing for a century, or so,
before finding something better
to do, other than jaw-achingly
backbreaking chew its own muck up –
is Scunthorpe.

Great crouched safety-
toecapped man, hidden
from German bombers
but not corner shopkeepers –
where is your heart of steel?

Is it in the battle just lost
without a lot of effort
to keep your furnaces open?

Or in the old frame rusting
away in the shed you used
to clock on, flock to work
to and fro from – with the verve
of birds in search of a better life.
Come climb on their wings and ride,
each rock-steady two-way migration flight?